**Circulation: Please
check for disc in back.**

D1263249

RED LIGHT, RED LIGHT, WHAT DO YOU SAY?

Retold by NICHOLAS IAN

Illustrated by DIEGO FUNCK

Music Arranged and Produced by MUSICAL YOUTH PRODUCTIONS

CANTATA
LEARNING

WWW.CANTATALEARNING.COM

CANTATA
LEARNING

Published by Cantata Learning
1710 Roe Crest Drive
North Mankato, MN 56003
www.cantatalearning.com

A note to educators and librarians from the publisher: Cantata Learning has provided the following data to assist in book processing and suggested use of Cantata Learning product.

Publisher's Cataloging-in-Publication Data
Prepared by Librarian Consultant: Ann-Marie Begnaud
Library of Congress Control Number: 2015958198
 Red Light, Red Light, What Do You Say?
 Series: Tangled Tunes : On the Move
 Retold by Nicolas Ian
 Illustrated by Diego Funck
 Summary: Sing about what traffic lights mean in this twist on a classic song.
 ISBN: 978-1-63290-601-4 (library binding/CD)
 ISBN: 978-1-63290-641-0 (paperback/CD)
Suggested Dewey and Subject Headings:
 Dewey: E 363.12
 LCSH Subject Headings: Electronic traffic controls – Juvenile literature. | Traffic safety – Juvenile literature. | Electronic traffic controls – Songs and music – Texts. | Traffic safety – Songs and music – Texts. | Electronic traffic control – Juvenile sound recordings. | Traffic safety – Juvenile sound recordings.
 Sears Subject Headings: Traffic safety. | Safety education. | School songbooks. | Children's music. | World music.
 BISAC Subject Headings: JUVENILE NONFICTION / Health & Daily Living / Safety. | JUVENILE NONFICTION / Music / Songbooks. | JUVENILE NONFICTION / Transportation / General.

Book design and art direction, Tim Palin Creative
Editorial direction, Flat Sole Studio
Music direction, Elizabeth Draper
Music arranged and produced by Musical Youth Productions

Printed in the United States of America in North Mankato, Minnesota.
072016   0335CGF16

Traffic lights help cars, trucks, and people move safely on city streets. They have three colored lights. One is red, one yellow, and one green. What does each color mean?

To find out, turn the page and sing along!

Green light, green light, what do you say?
Green light, green light, what do you say?

GO! GO! GO!

I tell the driver, "Go. Go right away!"
I tell the driver, "Go. Go right away!"

Yellow light, yellow light, what do you mean?
Yellow light, yellow light, what do you mean?

I mean wait till the light turns green!
I mean wait till the light turns green!

Red light, red light, what do you say?
Red light, red light, what do you say?

I tell the driver to stop right away!
I tell the driver to stop right away!

Red means stop. Yellow means slow.
Green means go, go, go!

Red means stop. Yellow means slow.
Green means go, go, go!

Green light, green light, what do you say?
Green light, green light, what do you say?

I tell the driver, "Go. Go right away!"
I tell the driver, "Go. Go right away!"

15

Yellow light, yellow light, what do you mean?
Yellow light, yellow light, what do you mean?

I mean wait till the light turns green!
I mean wait till the light turns green!

Red light, red light, what do you say?
Red light, red light, what do you say?

I tell the driver to stop right away!
I tell the driver to stop right away!

Red means stop. Yellow means slow.
Green means go, go, go!

Red means stop. Yellow means slow.
Green means go, go, go!

Thank you, thank you, red, yellow, and green.
Now I know what traffic lights mean!

SONG LYRICS
Red Light, Red Light, What Do You Say?

Green light, green light, what do you say?
Green light, green light, what do you say?

I tell the driver, "Go. Go right away!"
I tell the driver, "Go. Go right away!"

Yellow light, yellow light, what do you mean?
Yellow light, yellow light, what do you mean?

I mean wait till the light turns green!
I mean wait till the light turns green!

Red light, red light, what do you say?
Red light, red light, what do you say?

I tell the driver to stop right away!
I tell the driver to stop right away!

Red means stop. Yellow means slow.
    Green means go, go, go!
Red means stop. Yellow means slow.
    Green means go, go, go!

Green light, green light, what do you say?
Green light, green light, what do you say?

I tell the driver, "Go. Go right away!"
I tell the driver, "Go. Go right away!"

Yellow light, yellow light, what do you mean?
Yellow light, yellow light, what do you mean?

I mean wait till the light turns green!
I mean wait till the light turns green!

Red light, red light, what do you say?
Red light, red light, what do you say?

I tell the driver to stop right away!
I tell the driver to stop right away!

Red means stop. Yellow means slow.
    Green means go, go, go!
Red means stop. Yellow means slow.
    Green means go, go, go!

Thank you, thank you, red, yellow, and green.
Now I know what traffic lights mean!

Red Light, Red Light, What Do You Say?

Indie Pop (World/Folk)
Musical Youth Productions

Verse 2
Yellow light, yellow light, what do you mean?
Yellow light, yellow light, what do you mean?
I mean wait till the light turns green!
I mean wait till the light turns green!

Verse 3
Red light, red light, what do you say?
Red light, red light, what do you say?
I tell the driver to stop right away!
I tell the driver to stop right away!

Verse 4
Red means stop. Yellow means slow.
Green means go, go, go!
Red means stop. Yellow means slow.
Green means go, go, go!

Verse 5
Green light, green light, what do you say?
Green light, green light, what do you say?
I tell the driver, "Go. Go right away!"
I tell the driver, "Go. Go right away!"

Verse 6
Yellow light, yellow light, what do you mean?
Yellow light, yellow light, what do you mean?
I mean wait till the light turns green!
I mean wait till the light turns green!

Verse 7
Red light, red light, what do you say?
Red light, red light, what do you say?
I tell the driver to stop right away!
I tell the driver to stop right away!

Verse 8
Red means stop. Yellow means slow.
Green means go, go, go!
Red means stop. Yellow means slow.
Green means go, go, go!
Thank you, thank you, red, yellow, and green.
Now I know what traffic lights mean!

ACCESS THE MUSIC!
SCAN CODE WITH MOBILE APP
CANTATALEARNING.COM

23

GLOSSARY

green light—a traffic light that tells vehicles it is okay to go

red light—a traffic light that tells vehicles to stop

traffic—the movement of vehicles along a street

yellow light—a traffic light that tells vehicles to slow down and get ready to stop

GUIDED READING ACTIVITIES

1. Count the traffic lights on your ride to school. On a sheet of paper, tally how many were green, yellow, and red.

2. Traffic lights and stop signs keep people safe. What other kinds of signs help people stay safe? Draw a safety sign that you have seen in your neighborhood.

3. Think about the last time you were in a car, on a school bus, walking, or riding your bike. What did you do to stay safe?

TO LEARN MORE

Anderson, Steven. *Wheels on the Bus*. Mankato, MN: Cantata Learning, 2016.

Ipcizade, Catherine. *H Is for Honk! A Transportation Alphabet*. Mankato, MN: Capstone Press, 2011.

Lyons, Shelly. *Signs in My Neighborhood*. Mankato, MN: Capstone Press, 2013.

Lyons, Shelly. *Transportation in My Neighborhood*. Mankato, MN: Capstone Press, 2013.